Also By Brenda Hasse

<u>An Afterlife Journey Trilogy</u>
On The Third Day
From Beyond The Grave
Until We Meet Again

<u>Adult</u>
The Cursed Witch
Leaving You Behind
A Victim Of Desperation

<u>Young Adult</u>
The Freelancer
A Lady's Destiny
The Moment of Trust
Wilkinshire

<u>Picture Books For Children</u>
My Horsy And Me, What Can We Be?
A Unicorn For My Birthday
Yes, I Am Loved

The Fenton *Ghost Walk* Revisited

~

Brenda Hasse

The Fenton Ghost Walk Revisited

Copyright © 2022 by Brenda Hasse

All rights reserved. No part of the book may be used or reproduced by any means, graphic, electronic, or mechanical, including photocopying, recording, taping, or by any storage, information retrieving system without the permission of the publisher except in the case of brief quotations embodied in critical articles or reviews.

The characters in this novel are based on people in history, while others are fictional.

Because of the dynamic nature of the Internet and Web, addresses and links may have changed since publication and may no longer be valid.

All photographs and skits published in this novel were granted permission by the A. J. Phillips Fenton Museum, Fenton Historical Society, Fenton Ghost Walk Team, the author, host households, and touring guests. Cover photo by Colin Hodgkin.

979-8-9864383-1-3 (pb)

979-8-9864-383-2-0 (ebk)

To the Fenton Ghost Walk Team, Fenton Village Players, A. J. Phillips Fenton Museum, Fenton Historical Society, volunteers, and host households, whose hard work and effort made the Fenton Ghost Walk a 'spooktacular' success.

Index

Madam Chairmen	1
A. J. Phillips Fenton Museum	3
2014	4
2016	14
2017	26
2019	36
Scripts	50
Reunion Of Class Of '59	51
Stagecoach Stop And The Free Slave	58
Mr. & Mrs. Johnson And Elihu Waite	63
The Lost Child	69
Citizens Of Fentonville	
Israel Buzzard	74
David Colwell	75
Charles Fechenscher	76
Adelaide Fenon	78
Dexter Horton	79
Doctor Isaac Wixom, MD	81
The Famous Poker Game	82
Rena Conrad	86
101 Rockwell Street	90
711 South Leroy Street	94
308 South Holly Road	97
305 Rockwell Street	101
407 Pine Street	104
206 Rockwell Street	107
First Presbyterian Church	110
Jokes	112

The Fenton Ghost Walk
Madam Chairmen

Toadie Middleton   Bev Tippett

The Fenton Ghost Walk was chaired by Toadie Middleton and Bev Tippett. Its purpose was to raise funds for the Fenton Village Players and the Fenton Historical Society. Their dedication made each event a success and enjoyed by those who attended.

Andrew Jackson Phillips
1837 ~ 1904

Bottom Center
Marjorie Marshall Phillips
1898 ~ 1905

A. J. Phillips Fenton Museum

Every Fenton Ghost Walk tour began at the A. J. Phillips Fenton Museum, constructed in 1900. It was initially A. J. Phillips' private office until 1904. In 1906, it was donated to the City of Fenton for use as a library on the condition that it be well maintained, and no temperance meeting be conducted within its walls. It was the A. J. Phillips Library from 1906 to 1987. Some have claimed to see the ghost of Marjorie Phillips, A. J. Phillips' granddaughter, in the center top window. She is dressed in a white garment and clutches a teddy bear in the crook of her arm. Marjorie died at age seven.

2014 Photos

Civil War Soldier

Before leaving to fight in the Civil War, the men gathered at the town square, now known as Freedom Park. They would bid their loved ones farewell, promise to return, and wish them well as they departed.

Here is a list of the brave men of Fenton who were called to duty to fight in the Civil War.

Joseph W. Moore, Joel Dibble, Jonathan Terry, William Meginnes, Thomas Holland, Joseph W. Cole, Palmer Eldridge, George Hopkins, Cash M. Jones, George Ludlow, Charles S. Johnson, Ernest T. Winters, Jeremiah S. Knapp, F. Warren McComber, Clark T. Dibble, Charles Totten, Amsey Rogers, Daniel Varnum, Henry Osgood, Edward A. Morey, Edgar Durfee, John C. Thorpe, Charles T. Conrad, Edwin J. Hewitt, Henry C. Van Atta, John Owen, David S. Rich, Chauncey P. Ryno, Calvin L. Mann, Benjamin F. Marsh, Theodore Grimson, Henry O. Clark, William H. Giles, Clayton Taylor, James W. Perry, William E. Aldrich, Abner D. Swett, Isaac H. Lawrence, Ebin Remington, Albert E. Herrington, Ezra St. John, Marcello Barnum, George W. Case, Elias B. Wightman, Elbert A. Young, Andrew W. Holliday, Edward H. Dickerman, Moses Carr, Philander Linley, Newton B. Morris, Lemon B. Chappell, Charles F. Barber, George W. Barbour, George Adams, Benjamin Botsford, Asher E. Mather, John M. Wright, James Giles, Thomas G. Skelton, Charles F. Wortman, John Ganson, Enos Golden, Alfred Ganson, Amos K. Clark, Alvah H. Marsh, Lewis C. Ackerman, Joseph Cathcart, John W. Banks, Daniel C. Parker, Carpenter Kimball, Byron Vosburg, Frank Hanmer, Asa H. Fields, Laban Connor, Wilson P. Donaldson, James S. Robinson, Andrew Bly, Milo Crawford, Marion Munson, James W. Ripley, Charles Feckenscher, Edwin M. Hovey, Edward S. Hirst, Edward N. Bennett, Anson Morehouse, Lewis V. Curry, Thomas Clark, William Butcher, Edward F. Farnum, Seymour Thompson, Luke J. Tryon, Edwin Rogers, James A. Dunlap, Dexter Horton.

The Fenton Hotel

The Fenton Hotel was built in 1856. Dwight Wood DeNio was the 'hotel keeper' along with his wife, Estelle Westfall, and their two daughters, Anna and Etta. They lived on the third floor with their staff and renters of the working class.

This photo was taken of the Fenton Citizens Band before the DeNio House in 1885.

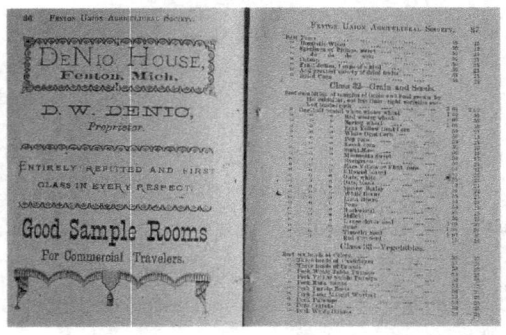

Spirits Of The Fenton Hotel

Many witnesses agree that some of the past guests in the hotel have never left.

They often hear footsteps walking on the floors above. Some believe it is Emery, the hotel's old custodian, pacing in his old room where he passed away.

Beware when using the ladies' restroom. The ghost of a young lady is often seen in the third stall. Legend has it she had an affair with a patron, became pregnant, and hung herself in that stall.

Bartenders often report a gentleman at table 32 who orders a glass of whiskey. When they go to serve the drink, the man has vanished.

Disembodied voices, being touched by an unseen hand, and moving glassware is nothing new to this old establishment.

Billmeier Camera Shop

The Billmeier Camera Shop resided at 100 South Leroy Street. Established in 1958, it developed a reputation as a business that knew everything about cameras.

Does his spirit still reside within the walls of his beloved business?

Workers At The A. J. Phillips Factory

The photo of the A. J. Phillips Factory was taken in 1890. It was three and a half acres of floor space and covered twelve acres of land in the heart of Fenton. It produced wooden pumps, wooden shovels, and milk safes. Sometime in the early 1880s, Phillips invented the sliding window screen. Legend indicates his sliding window screens were installed in the White House.

Underground Railroad

Fenton played an important part in the underground railroad. The house at 825 Sinclair Street is said to have offered shelter to runaway slaves. It was on Route #6. To keep the escaped slaves hidden from the authorities when they came to call, the residents would rush them through a trap door in the living room floor to hide beneath, place a rug over the passage, and the grandmotherly woman would sit in a rocking chair, rock, and sing to an invisible infant held within her arms. Her singing helped to cover up any noise the slaves may make. It also convinced the authorities that she was not quite right in her mind, a bit off her rocker so to speak.

First Presbyterian Church
The Horton Sisters

Two sisters, Mrs. Myra Bussey and Mrs. Mary A. Rackham, were instrumental in overseeing updates to the First Presbyterian Church in 1930 in honor of their mother, Mrs. Dexter Horton. They are credited for remodeling the parlors, dining room, kitchen, and installing a new heating system. In 1935, the congregation voted to purchase a new organ and much-needed carpet. Mrs. Bussey stepped forward and saw the impossible task completed through her donation. Occasionally, a single key on the organ will play. Some say it is the ghost of Mrs. Bussey reminding everyone that nothing is impossible, and she is nearby and still watching over the church.

2016

Mr. & Mrs. A. J. Phillips

In 1861, A. J. Phillips married Julie Bullard. They moved to Milford the following year. In 1869, they came to Fenton with their three sons. Mr. Phillips set up and expanded his factory over the years. Rumors suggest that he also liked to indulge in his favorite alcoholic beverage, which Mrs. Phillips was against. In fact, she would hold temperance meetings in his business office, now Yesterday's Treasures. Having had enough of her prodding and interruptions with the gaggle of gossiping women when they gathered, he distanced himself by building his private office, which is now the A. J. Phillips Fenton Museum. Poor Mrs. Phillips, whose spirit stands in the business office window weeping for her husband to give up his wayward drinking.

Civil War Sweethearts

Alvah Blood and Effie Tombs were sweethearts before the Civil War. Being called to duty, Alvah left the love of his life with the promise of returning. Throughout the war, they kept in contact through letters. After Abraham Lincoln's assassination, Alvah accompanied the President's body on the train to Illinois. He then walked home to Fenton. Shortly afterward, he married Effie. After the ceremony, they climbed into their horse-drawn wagon and sped away, so happy to finally be together. However, they took a turn too quickly, the wagon tipped over, and they were both killed.

King Fisher

King Fisher lived in Mundy Township. He was tall and described as a Caucasian savage man who married a local native American, began a family, grew corn, and lived near Lack Copneconic. King Fisher donned his head with a top hat, his self-proclaiming crown. He visited Mrs. Benjamin Rockwell, William M. Fenton's sister, who owned a beautifully carved harpsichord piano. Both Mrs. Rockwell and Mrs. Fenton were present during his visit. After listening to the instrument being played, he stated it was a 'good spirit' and asked Mrs. Rockwell to dance. She refused.

Reunion Of The Class Of '59

On Thursday, June 29, 1909, a group of women from the Fenton High School Class of 1859 gathered at Miss Mercie Thompson's residence for a lovely luncheon. She had beautifully decorated it in the class colors of red, white, and blue. During their 50th reunion, the women reminisced about the first day of school when they rose early, wore their best dress, did their chores, and walked to school. Once in their classroom, they sang 'Lightly Row." They discussed their favorite subjects, where the school buildings were located in town, classmates, and past crushes on boys. (see script)

2016 Photos

Stagecoach Stop And
The Free Slave

On the corner of Shiawassee and Adelaide is a house formerly used as a stagecoach stop. It was known as stop No. VII. Stop No. VI is how the city of Novi acquired its name. The actors performed on the porch of the Melrose House at 114 West Shiawassee Avenue. The couple, Mr. & Mrs. Melrose, discussed the stagecoach and Miss Libby, owner of the brothel, located directly behind the stagecoach stop. Much to their surprise, James joined them on the porch. He described his escape from slavery and entertained them as he sang a few songs. He was pleased President Lincoln had signed the Emancipation Proclamation, which did not free slaves but made it possible for Union Soldiers to take them northward to freedom. With the help of others, James distanced himself from captivity and was relieved to cross the Mason-Dixon line, but his troubles were not over. If his owner tracked him down, he would be returned. But for now, he sang his song of freedom. (see script)

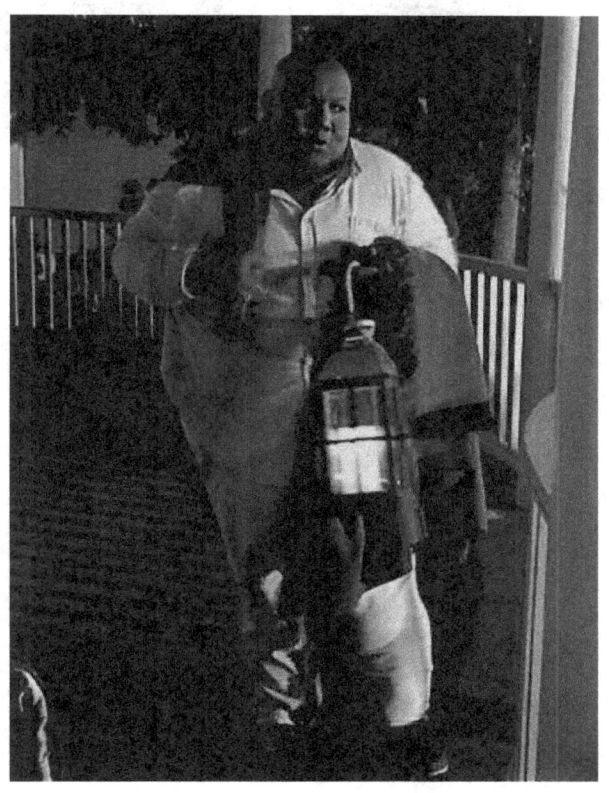

Mr. & Mrs. Johnson and Elihu Waite

In 1872, Mr. and Mrs. Johnson owned a crockery store at 105 West Shiawassee Avenue in the Andrews Building, constructed in 1867. They sold dishware, flatware, crystal, and tea sets, just to name a few items. Mrs. Johnson was also a hat maker (milliner) and stocked an ample supply. They shared the Andrew Building with three other businesses; Booth and Boutell, who sold books, jewelry, and music, A. Curtiss Clothier, and E. N. Chandler Hardware and Detroit Stoves. The second floor was occupied by the Fenton Independent, a reputable newspaper, and the Ladies Library Association.

Mr. Elihu Waite interruptions Mr. Johnson to explain that he once owned a hardware store in the same location, now Fenton's Open Book. Elihu is a resident ghost who likes to knock books from the shelves. While a resident of Fenton, he was the justice of the peace, married to Elizabeth Tarbell, and had seven lovely children. Upon his wife's death, he went to live with his sons for a time before returning to Fenton, marrying Myra Thompkinson, and opening a hardware store. He became senile toward the end of his 85 years and succumbed to grippe (flu). His second wife passed away three months later. Because of his senility, Eli's spirit thinks he still owns and operates his hardware store and often makes his presence known. (see script)

The Presbyterian Church Bell

In 1862, The Board of Church Erection obtained a loan of $500. A year later, a wooden building for the Presbyterian Church was built using one-inch-thick boards that were twelve inches wide, and strips of battens covered the cracks between the boards. In 1864, the congregation raised money to pay for a bell for the steeple. A company in Pennsylvania forged the iron bell, shipped it by train, and placed it in the steeple. If you observe the bell's clapper today, it is worn on one side, indicating the bellringers had difficulty pulling the rope to swing it enough to strike both sides.

2016 Photos

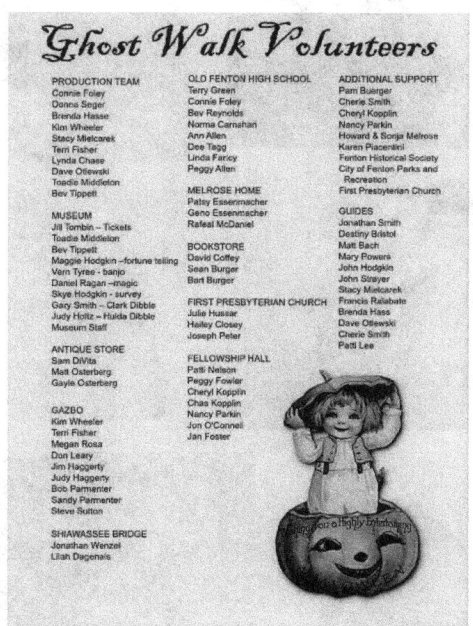

2017

Joseph Smallbone

Joseph Milo Smallbone, a mysterious and eccentric individual, dressed in black. His face was soot-streaked from the wood stove used to heat his house on Wakeman Street, where he lived with his mother until her death. He owned two Model A cars and was a handyman who fixed radios and TVs. Those who encountered him could not help but notice his unkept and unwashed appearance. He often rode a bike. Nevertheless, he was a legend in his own time.

The Lost Child

In the early days of Dibbleville, Clark Dibble traveled to Grumlaw (Grand Blanc) and convinced three families to move to his newly purchased 40 acres and resettle. The Cheney family agreed. They build a log cabin on the corner of Shiawassee and Adelaide, where the A. J. Phillips's house now resides. It was cramped quarters for the family of nine and rough living off the land. Mrs. Dustin Cheney had taken several of her older children with her to search for suitable land to plant corn. Young Louise wanted to tag along, but her mother sent her back to the cabin. Unfortunately, she wandered off the trail and became lost. People searched for Louise for three days, but they could not find her.

Mr. Winchell, who worked at Clark Dibble's mill, had retired for the evening after a hard day's work. He woke from a dream at 2:00 AM and went to the spot he had seen in his dream. He discovered Louise there. She had stayed close to a puddle of water. He carried her home to her mother. (see script)

Citizens of Fenton

Many of Fenton's citizens served or were affected by the Civil War. The men mustered at the town square, now Freedom Park. Their loved ones watched them depart, not knowing if they would ever see them alive again. Several soldiers and citizens shared their contributions to the cause. Those who stepped forward and spoke were Israel Buzzard, David Colwell, Charles Feckenscher, Adelaide Fenton, Dexter Horton, and Doctor Isaac Wixom, MD. Please read their scripts for their individual contributions. (see scripts)

The Brothel

There were once three brothels within Fenton; one on Second Street, a house behind the stagecoach building, and one said to be on the second floor of the Andrews Building. One male customer's visit to his favorite lady became widely known. He hung his pants on the bedpost and when he put them back on, he discovered his money had been stolen. He alerted the authorities. Unfortunately, the crime was reported in the local paper making him the laughingstock of the town. During their stops at the depot, many railroad workers would visit the brothels. Accompanied with a red lens lantern, they could be easily located at departure time. This gave a brothel the nickname 'the redlight district.'

The Famous Poker Game

In 1834, Clark Dibble purchased a 40 acre parcel from the government. In 1837, he sold the settlement of Dibbleville to William Fenton, Robert LeRoy, and Benjamin Rockwell. They wanted to rename the town and decided to let the cards of a poker game determine who the town would be named after. Fenton had the highest hand, so he named his newly acquired town Fentonville, which was later changed to Fenton in 1963. LeRoy, who placed second, had his name proudly displayed on the main street, and Rockwell, the lowest hand, is the name of the residential street. The game is rumored to have been played at the house at 609

Leroy Street. Some believe the game was played in LeRoy's hotel. (see script)

First Presbyterian Church
Rena Conrad

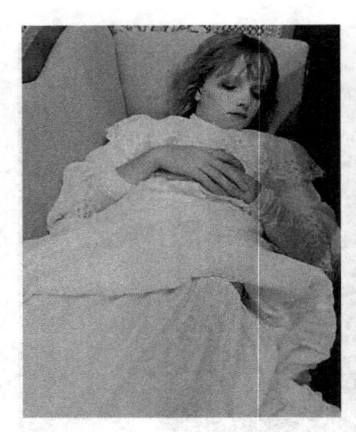

Reverend Work reenacts the eulogy of Rena Conrad, a young resident of Fenton who passed away at nineteen years of age. She suffered from rheumatism, which affected her heart. The young lady was a junior at Fenton High School. She was very popular, described as having a sunny, cheerful disposition, and an active participant in the First Presbyterian Church. When many were cared for in their home, Rena's father was also ill, so she was taken to L. M. Cook's house, a neighbor and druggist across the street, where she passed away. The service was concluded with the song 'Beautiful Isle of Somewhere.' Fellow classmates carried her casket. (see script)

2017 Photos

2019

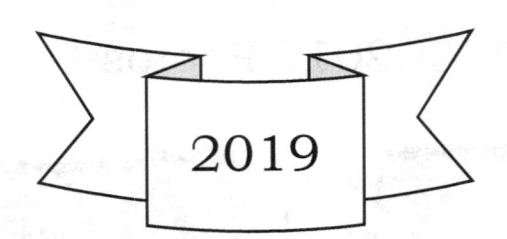

101 Rockwell Street

The house on the corner of Rockwell and Leroy has been long known as the Honey House. John Hamilton built the house in 1902. His wife, Charlotte, grew beautiful flowers and kept bees. The jars of honey they produced were handed out to children at Halloween. After their passing, their son, Chester, inherited the house. During the cold winter months, he allowed Miss Alice Van Atta to teach piano lessons in the front room. The present owner has experienced the upstairs shower turning on by itself and books pushed toward the back of the shelf. Her dog will not go into the basement. Can the canine detect the unseen spirits? (see script)

711 South Leroy Street

On the corner of Leroy and South Holly is a house built by James E. Bussey. He and his wife, Mary, and their five children lived there before moving to the Coe's house on the corner of South Holly and East Street. Bussey's house was purchased by widowed Mary Wells Eddy. Loneliness was unwelcomed company for Mrs. Eddy. She invited her niece, Miss Maude Morris, to live with her, and she accepted. They often shared an afternoon tea together. After Mrs. Eddy's passing, Morris inherited the house. She would set out tea for two and sit before the front window, just in case someone should stop by. (see script)

South Ward School

This is the South Ward School built in 1879. It sat at South Holly Road and East Street. It was a square, brick building with one large room downstairs and one large room upstairs. A potbellied stove was the heat source, and it had an outside bathroom. This was the elementary school.

The South Ward School was built in 1864. It was a two-story brick building, located at the corner of South Holly Street and East Street. It housed third and fourth grade classes. There were 28 to 40 students in each class. The students would attend school from 8:00 AM to 4:00 PM and have an hour for lunch. Their source of heat during the winter months was a potbelly coal stove. With no running water inside the building, their restrooms consisted of two outhouses, one labeled 'girls' and the other labeled 'boys.' They were located at the far end of the playground. To use the restroom, a student had to raise their hand with either one finger or two, indicating the 'business' they needed to address. The hall pass was a rock on the teacher's desk. Students had to wade through the snow in the winter to use the outhouse, which deterred many from taking a restroom break. Since there were no busses, students walked to school, and unfriendly dogs were always a hazard. Red signs near the sidewalk indicated an illness within the home. Class was not held during the spring (planting time) or fall (harvest time). Students began attending school at age six. They went directly to first grade, no kindergarten back then. Two other schools in Fenton were the North Ward School on the corner of Second and East Streets and West Ward, which was attached to the high school on Ellen Street.

1923 North Ward School

308 South Holly Street

This home was built in 1870 by Charles W. Coe. He and his wife, Anne, raised a daughter, Mary, who married James E. Bussey. Bussey added the Victorian features of the inherited house. Coe fought in the Civil War under the command of Brigadier General George Armstrong Custer at the Battle of Gettysburg. His granddaughter, Grace Bussey Gurnea, a young widow, resided with Mary Bussey until her death. Today's residents say they often hear furniture being moved in adjacent rooms. A rosary and business journal were discovered in a wall of the house while doing some renovations. One woman claimed to watch a man dressed in uniform, standing at attention, next to a casket and people entering through the north door and exiting through a second door that is no longer there. This is assumed to be the residual reoccurrence of Charles Coe's funeral visitation. Two small cement caskets were unearthed when the garage was added to the house. One has the word 'Baby' decoratively written with stones on the top. Whether a child or a beloved pet is inside, no one really knows. (see script)

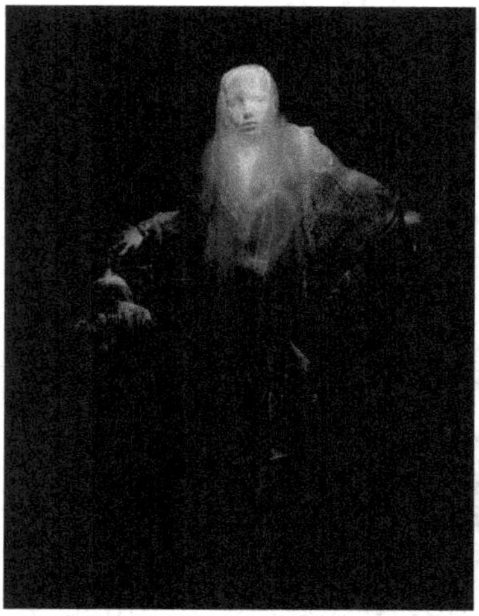
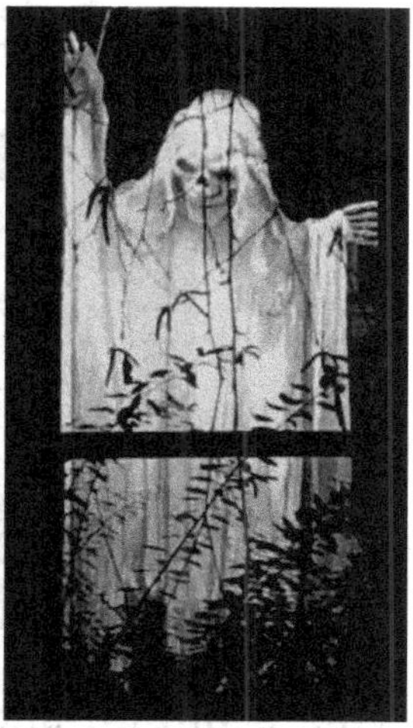
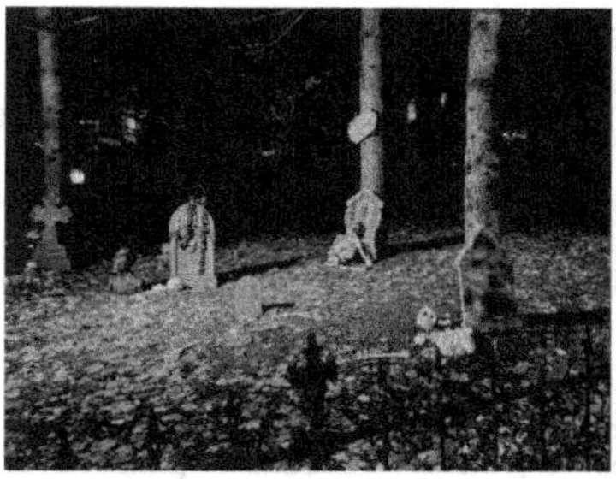
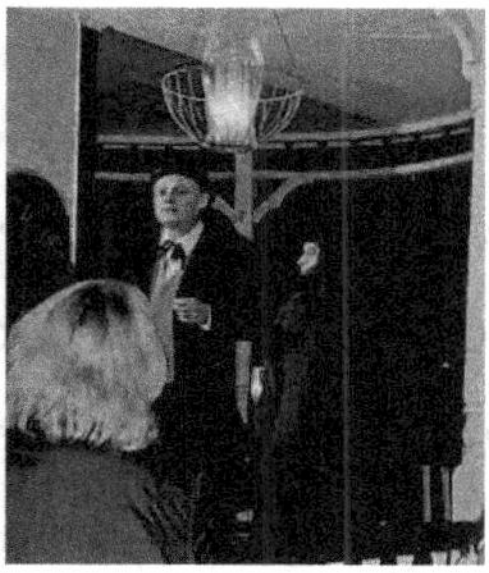
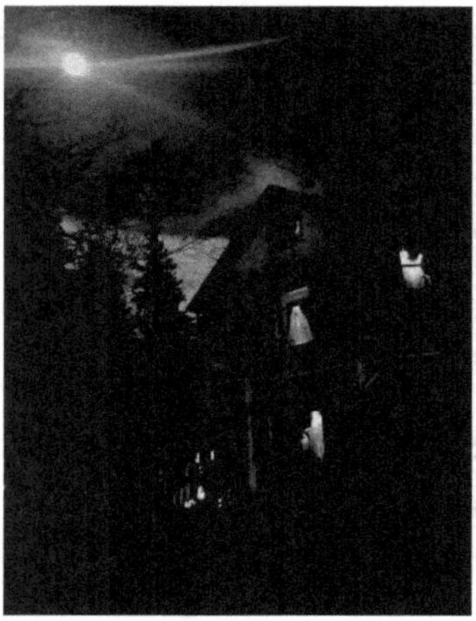
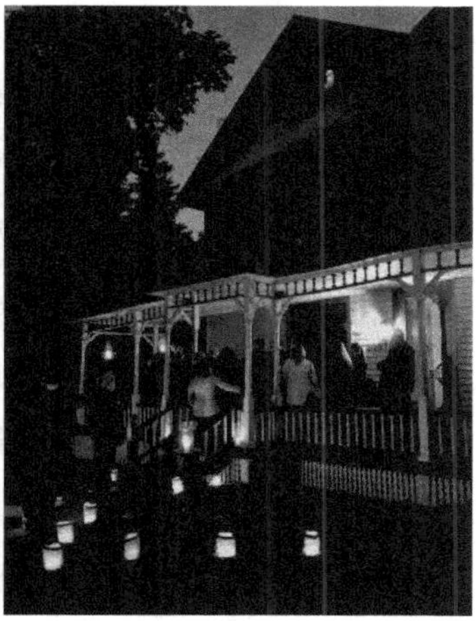

305 Rockwell Street

This beautiful and uniquely designed house was built in 1860 by James R. Burdick Potter. He owned a saddlery and harness business in town. Another resident was Fritz E. Jeudevine. Fritz worked in his family's local grocery and meat market. The current resident of this house has seen an apparition of a pair of men's pants in the dining room as she exited the kitchen. The owner has also had her hair pulled while watching TV. On one occasion, she forgot to blow out a candle before retiring for the night. When she rose the following morning, it had been extinguished. She suspects the resident ghost of Horace Carter Churchill. He owned and lived in the house for many years. Horace was taken advantage of by his caretaker. She refused to pay back the money he loaned her and claimed he was senile. (see script)

407 Pine Street

This grand old house was built in the 1860s by John Dedrick. He secured a loan from Henry Clay Riggs, who can attest that the cost did not break the bank. Henry, a druggist, and attorney at law, personally loaned John the money. However, the competitive battle between bank owners Ewin Trump and George Washington Wilmot did break the bank. They owned the Trump Wilmot Bank and decided to have a competition to see who could build the most beautiful house. Wilmot's big white house is located on the southeast corner of East Street and Rockwell Street. Trump's house is on the southeast corner of High Street and East Street. They look very similar in architecture. Trump's house is larger and once had a gym on the third floor. (see script)

206 Rockwell Street

This is the tale of a love story that ended in tragedy and embezzlement. Augustus St. Amand, originally from France, married Caroline LeRoy, sister of Robert LeRoy. They lived in the house at 206 Rockwell Street and had four children. Caroline passed away in an upstairs bedroom eleven days after giving birth to her daughter, who died at three months of age. Augustus remarried Emily Stene and had four children. Augustus was the Treasurer of Genesee County. He mysteriously left his job and went to France. It was discovered that funds had been taken from the county. Mr. Robert L. Sheldon and Col. William M. Fenton replaced the amount that was stolen. (see script)

Christian Science

Sara Gallup Phillips, wife of Winfield B. Phillips and daughter-in-law to Mr. and Mrs. A. J. Phillips, introduced Christian Science to Fenton in the 1890s. They held their meetings and Sunday lessons/sermons at various locations within Fenton for many years. In January 1937, a donation from the Horace H. and Mary Rackham Fund provided the funds for the building located at 204 East Rockwell Street. Horace Rackham was the accountant for Henry Ford and a stockholder in the Ford Motor Company. Ford bought him out for $18,000,000. The Rackhams also provided funds for the Fenton Community Center and Fenton Fire Hall. They were residents of Detroit before moving to Fenton.

First Presbyterian Church

This lovely ghostly guide conveyed the struggle of our country and city during the Civil War. Fentonville was one of many stops along the Underground Railroad. 'Conductors' would guide escaped slaves northward. 'Stations' or 'depots' described the hiding places for slaves. A 'station master' was someone who would hide a runaway slave. An escaped slave was often referred to as 'cargo,' 'fleece,' 'a passenger,' and 'freight.' 'Freedom trails' referred to the route to the 'promised land' known as freedom. (see script)

2019 Photos

Thank You Volunteers

Spooky Steering Committee
Connie Foley-Historian
Brenda Haase - Storywriter
Toadie Middleton- Co-chair
Stacey Mielcarek - Advertising
Bev Tippett -Co-chair

Ghostly Guides
John Hodgkin & Skye Hodgkin
Stacey Mielcarek & Francis Ralabate
Jonathan Smith & Daniel Ragan
Brooke Lamson & Rhonda Young
Mickey & Morgan VIzard & Steve Sutton
Brenda Hasse & Denise Griffin

Appraitions
Bart & Sean Burger
Robbie Carnes
Karen Craner
Sam DiVIta
Linda Faricy
Connie Foley
Brent Griffin
Annadelle Kimber-Smith
Don Leary
Megan Rosa
Sean Sage
Cherie Smith
Nolan Splavec

Hauntingly Wonderful Hosts
Donna & Ryan Brogan
Elizabeth Dickens
Mark & Jan Blough
Dennis & Megan Putman
Ken & Donna Seger
John & Michelle Hillis
First Church of Christ, Scientist

Hocus Pocus Hospitality
Fenton First Presbyterian Church
Cheryl Kopplin
Chas Kopplin
Nancy Parkin

Mysterious Volunteers
Karen Anderson
Julie Hussar
Donna Lloyd
Holly Hodgkin
Maggie Hodgkin
Karey Sage
Kim Wheeler
Verne Tryee
John, Teaghan, Aiden, Rowan Sage & Emilie Poirer
Bryan & Jacci Thayer
Lisa Vaugn & Youth Strings from the Fenton Orchestra

Scripts

Reunion Of The Class Of '59

Cast:

Mrs. Ella Sheldon Latourette (recording secretary)
Mrs. Lucinda Smith Mason (treasurer)
Mrs. Libbie Hadley Devine (executive committee – from Holly)
Mrs. Ela Walton Russell (president)
Mrs. Libbie Denton Hadley (vice president)
Mrs. Dillah Brown Welch (executive committee – from Rose)
Miss Mercie Thompson (hostess of reunion)
Mrs. Jennie Reynolds Mahaney (executive committee – from Owosso)
Mr. Deveraunx (photographer)

Scene:

This is a recreation of a photograph taken by Mr. Deveraunx of the FHS Class of 1859 at their 50th class reunion in June of 1909. It is presently being performed in front of the Ellen Street Campus School on Adelaide Street.

Props:

Three chairs and a camera circa 1909

Deveraunx: Ladies, if you will, please bear with me while I set up. It will take just a moment. *(Fidgets with camera while ladies are huddled together to one side of the chairs while waiting to be posed for the photograph.)*

Russel: Mercie, on behalf of all of us, we want to thank you for the lovely luncheon. You have been an excellent hostess. I am impressed with the meticulous detail you have given in decorating your cherry dining room with flowers in our class colors of red, white, and blue. It was nice to have your two nieces serve the meal so that you could enjoy it equally.

Thompson: Thank you, but the pleasure is all mine.

Hadley: I must admit, it is simply delightful getting together to reminisce about old times. To think we graduated from Fenton High School fifty years ago, it seems as if time has flown by since the day we descended the stairs from the second floor as the class of 1859.

Devine: I remember with fondness our first day of school. I would rise before dawn to do my chores, dress, and walk to school, hoping to arrive early to visit with everyone before class began at 8:45. It was always exciting to be together again after the summer break. We would admire each other's new dresses, our hair was prinked and arranged perfectly, we carried our lunch tins, sat in our favorite seats, and giggled and whispered as we looked to see the new boys in our classroom.

Hadley: And singing 'Lightly Row."

Thompson: I hated that song. Even now, it echoes hauntingly in my mind.

Devine: While I was in town, I bought a copy of the Fenton Independent and came across an article featuring our school. It had received its accreditation sometime after we graduated. I am uncertain of the year, though.

Russel: Oh, I read that article too. They said that Fenton High School received the honor in 1875, and it was one of only five schools with such an accreditation in the state. It also went on to say that our school was recently placed on the approved school list for the University of Michigan for three years, the longest ever granted to any school.

Mason: There has been a lot of change in the district since we graduated. With so many people moving into the area, the high school underwent an expansion, and the two ward schools grew to the point of being so overcrowded that a room in the Andrews block had to be rented.

Welch: Why am I drawing a blank? I guess it has been a while since I have lived here. Refresh my memory. Where are the ward schools?

Latourette: One on the corner of North East and Second streets and the other on South East and South Holly.

Welch: Oh, that's right.

Latourette: The original ward buildings were torn down, and larger ones were built on the same sites. The curriculum has remained much of the same, though. They tried to remove the Latin and Greek classes, but the vote failed.

Mason: I didn't care much for Latin or Greek. I always struggled in those classes.

Russel: I liked Algebra, Geometry, and University Algebra most of all. Trigonometry and Surveying piqued my interest as well.

Hadley: My favorite were Astronomy, Chemistry, Geology, and Botany.

Thompson: It is interesting to see the pathways our lives have taken. I am very pleased and thankful for those of you who have endured the journey for our reunion. Jennie, you came all of the way from Owosso, Dillah from Rose, and Libbie from Holly. It is nice that every one of you is happily married with children and grandchildren. Simply wonderful. I, however, have remained single all of these years.

Mahaney: Not that you didn't have any takers. The boys were always chasing after you.

Thompson: Oh, I had chasers all right, but none worth their weight in salt to allow any of them to catch me. I guess the right man just didn't come along.

Mason: Well, you know what they say, "It's never too late."

Russel: I remember the boy who was quite sweet on you. He was a foreign pupil from the next district over. He would try to sit next to you in the library too.

Thompson: Oh, yes, Jimmy. He was tall and cute, but a bully and always in trouble. I assumed he had been kicked out of his school for bad behavior, and his parents paid for him to attend our school. He used to sit behind me during Latin Grammar class. I will never forget the day he dipped my braid into his inkwell, turning the tip black. When I leaned forward to yank it out of his hand, it splatted onto the back of my printed cotton dress and left a stain. Even countless washings wouldn't take it out. Since it was my new dress, my mother was quite angry to see it damaged. The teacher had Jimmy switch desks with someone in the front of the class so I wouldn't have to endure any more of his antics.

Russel: I remember it was close to our 4:00 dismissal time when it happened. The superintendent sauntered into our classroom. Since his office was adjacent to our room, I imagine he was curious about the cause of the ruckus. After talking with our teacher, the expression on his face was one of displeasure. He ordered Jimmy into the hallway. I'm certain their conversation wasn't a pleasant one. As I recall, you made sure that your admirer received his day of comeuppance. *(giggle)*

Thompson: Oh, yes. I made him a wonderful lunch for the very next day. I spread old lard on the slice of bread and made sure it was very thick. I didn't squeeze the juice out of the pickle so that the bread was soggy, and I included a wedge of moldy cheese and a shriveled, dried-out apple. Since we gals always ate our lunch together outside under the oak tree in the fall, I was unaware of his failure to bring a lunch to school every day. I thought he would get the message and quit bothering me, but my plan backfired. He ate the whole thing. I think he did it to prove how much he liked me.

Russel: I remember that day. Our lunchtime was from noon until 1:00. We giggled and cringed as we watched him eat it. It made me gag, so I had to turn my back toward him to be able to stomach my lunch.

Mahaney: I don't remember any of that happening.

Latourette: Me either. What happened after that?

Thompson: Since he was either thick-headed or blinded by love, he didn't understand my subtle hint. I finally had to tell him, quite bluntly, that I didn't want him as a boyfriend, just a friend. It must have hurt his feelings because he quit talking to me after our one-sided conversation.

Welch: Does anyone remember the name of our teacher?

Hadley: Taft? Wasn't it Doctor Taft?

Thompson: Yes, it was Doctor Taft, and he was also the pastor of the Baptist Church in town too.

Deveraunx: All right, ladies. Miss Thompson, since you are the hostess of this gathering, I shall have you take the center seat. *(Thompson sits.)* As president, Mrs. Russel, I need you to sit on her right. *(Russel sits.)* Mrs. Hadley, as vice president, you may sit on her left. *(Hadley sits.)* Everyone else file in behind them. *(Looks at the ladies' placement, returns to his camera.)* Eyes on me. *(No smiling for the photograph.)* Ready. *(flash.)*

Stagecoach Stop And The Free Slave

Cast:

Wife – the owner of Melrose house
Husband – the owner of Melrose house
James – freed slave (actor may wish to use a slave/southern dialect)

Scene:

Husband and wife are sitting in rocking chairs on the porch of the Melrose house. James is hiding on the west side of the house, awaiting his queue.

Props:

Two rocking chairs.

Wife: My, oh my, the town is lively today.

Husband: Maybe news came in on the stagecoach this afternoon. Ever since it arrived, I've noticed more and more people gathering in the town square. (*points finger in the direction of Freedom Park*) Maybe something was posted on the board, and people are reading it.

Wife: Even the brothel is unusually noisy for this time of day.

Husband: Miss Libby wakes her gals up just before the stagecoach arrives. They lure in the tired gentlemen after their long, dusty journey for a little personal entertainment. (*devilish smile upon his face*) She makes sure they have a splendid time. (*wife is silent. He looks at her. She is glaring at him. His smile disappears from his face. He clears his throat and speaks in a serious tone.*) Or so I have been told.

James: (*singing, emerges from the west side of the house and walks to the steps of the front porch*)

Husband: Hey there. (*James stops singing*) You shouldn't be out and about at this time of day.

James: I am a free man. President Lincoln signed the Emancipation Proclamation setting all of us slaves free.

Wife: Signed the what?

James: The Emancipation Proclamation. It is a document that has set all of us slaves free.

Husband: Free, you say. You look as if you have traveled afar.

James: Yes, sir. I was born on a plantation in Georgia. Mama caught a fever and died after a severe beating. Not quite sure who my daddy is or if he is alive. Many of my brothers and sisters were sold off. A group of us slaves got fed up with the mistreatment, so we ran away. We would travel northward using the stars at night as we waded through swamps, dodged trees in thick woods, and crossed fields. Bounty hunters would track us with their dogs. Some of us were caught, but most of us managed to escape. We eventually found a conductor. We could identify the safe houses by looking for a star on the gable or a black jockey statue with a lit lantern out front of a house. Many fine people risked their lives for us. Who knows what would have happened to them if they had gotten caught? I count my blessings. I am so very thankful for their effort.

<u>Wife</u>: So, you traveled by foot all of the way from Georgia to Fenton?

<u>James</u>: No, mam, once we found the first conductor, he arranged for our transportation to the next leg of the journey. The second gentleman bypassed a town where many escaped slaves had settled, knowing they were safe and welcomed. The town was in one of the Carolinas. There was a bad case of syphilis spreading within the settlement. The doctors there were supposed to be helping them get better. But that was not the case. They were using them as an experiment. Maybe they were trying to learn from them. I don't rightly know, but I was pretty thankful to avoid that part of the country.

<u>Wife</u>: (*wrinkles nose in disgust*) I'd be thankful to him too. No use in getting caught in a situation like that.

<u>Husband</u>: So, how did you arrive in Fenton?

<u>James</u>: It was a long, hard journey that took a few months, maybe even three. The few of us that

traveled together were known as 'cargo,' at least that is what the conductors called us. Sometimes we would have to hide for a week or two until it was safe for us to travel to the next conductor. We traveled through Kentucky, Ohio, and into Michigan. Word had reached the authorities in Detroit of our escape, so it wasn't safe for us to cross from there into Canada. Blacks are free in Canada, so most of us go there. The conductor in charge split us up. I was taken north through Adrian, Ann Arbor, and ended up here. He took me to the house west of the coach stop. (*point to the house west of the stagecoach house*) I was hidden in the cellar under the living room. The authorities visited a few times, but the kind, old woman who lives there, would place a rug over the trap door, sit in a rocking chair, and sing to an imaginary baby to cover up any noise we may make.

<u>Wife</u>: We? There were more than just you hiding?

<u>James</u>: Yes, mam. We were packed in so tightly that some were taken to the barn across the street and others went through tunnels to other houses in town.

<u>Husband</u>: Now that you are free, what will you do?

<u>James</u>: I don't rightly know, sir. I was supposed to have a conductor take me to Port Huron and cross into Canada, but I don't know where to find him. In truth, there is little reason for him to help me now.

<u>Wife</u>: (*she touches her husband's arm to get his attention*) He has nowhere to go. Do you think we could offer him a spot in the barn to lay his head at

night and meals in exchange for work that needs to be done around here?

<u>Husband</u>: You read my thoughts. (*addresses James*) Until you can decide where you want to go and how you will get there, you can stay in our barn, help us with work around here, and we will provide your meals. We might be able to pay you a small wage as well.

<u>James</u>: Thank you, sir, mam. Your kindness is appreciated.

<u>Wife</u>: What is your name?

<u>James</u>: James, mam. My name is James.

<u>Wife</u>: Breakfast is served at the crack of dawn, James.

<u>James</u>: Yes, mam. Thank you, kindly. (actor sings while walking toward the barn)

Mr. & Mrs. Johnson and Elihu Waite

Cast:

Mr. Johnson (owner of M & M Johnson & Company – crockery store)
Mrs. Johnson (millinery and wife)
Mr. Elihu (el-ee-hoo) Waite (prominent Fenton resident)

Scene:

In building #3 of the Andrews Block (aka: Fenton's Open Book).

Props:

None

Mr. Johnson: Welcome to our crockery store. I'm Mr. Johnson, the owner of M & M Johnson and Company. This is my wife (*He presents his wife. Mrs. Johnson smiles and nods her head in acknowledgment.*), and I'm confident we have a style of dishware to fit your everyday or special occasion needs. We also carry flatware. May I suggest a lovely tea set? (*looks to guests for a response*) No, perhaps dishes for your table? (*waits for a reply a moment*) Ah, maybe some crystal glasses for entertaining. I have a charming set that just arrived from England with every piece in perfect condition.

Mrs. Johnson: (*places her hand on his arm to interrupt*) My dear, maybe some of the lovely ladies are looking for a new hat. I make the finest in town.

Mr. Johnson: (*looks over the audience with a contemplative expression and speaks to his wife*) No, there isn't a familiar face in the bunch. I believe they are lost. (*addresses audience*) Well, let me be of service then. You are in the Andrews Block, constructed in 1867. We opened our business in 1872. This is unit number three. In unit number one (*point to the east*) is Booth and Boutell. They sell books, jewelry, and music. A. Curtiss Clothier is in unit number two. In unit number four (*point to the west*) is E. N. Chandler Hardware and Detroit Stoves. Upstairs is the Fenton Independent, a very reputable newspaper indeed, and the Ladies Library Association has an office upstairs as well.

Waite: Oh my, don't bore the people, Johnson. (*Waite steps forward from the back of the room. Mr. & Mrs. Johnson roll their eyes.*)

Mr. Johnson: I'm not boring them. I am informing them of the businesses in the Andrews Block.

Mrs. Johnson: Yes, we are trying to help them. They seem to be lost.

Waite: Then you may want to start by telling them the truth. You two know as well as I do that our businesses no longer exist. All that remains are these four walls. (*Motions to the walls with his hands.*)

Mr. Johnson: And our spirits that reside within them.

Waite: Along with the memories of our past lives that we hold dear.

Mrs. Johnson: We are aware of your contributions to our community. Perhaps you would like to share them with our guests.

Waite: As I look back, I admit I did leave my mark upon this good city.

Mr. Johnson: If you are going to tell your life history, Elihu. You might as well tell it from the beginning.

Waite: It may take some time to thoroughly explain.

Mrs. Johnson: We're dead and have an eternity to listen to your story, but these good people may need to move along soon. So, a shortened version would be appreciated.

Waite: Very well. On my mother's side, well, she was a Brewster, and they came over on the Mayflower. I am a descendent from a long line of New England ancestry, and my forefathers fought in the Revolutionary War. I was born in 1830 in Monroe County, New York. I moved to Michigan with my parents and brother. At age 16, I worked on a farm for $50 a year. I saved my pay to rent some land in Rose Township and used the profits from my two years of farming to purchase 80 acres of land in Tyrone Township. I built a house and cultivated the land. When I was 20 years old, I married my wife, Elizabeth Tarbell. We had seven lovely children together.

Mrs. Johnson: But you were more than a farmer to the community. Go on, tell them.

Waite: You know I don't like to brag. I put my family on a higher pedestal than my accomplishments.

Mr. Johnson: We know. We have heard your story a few times before.

Mrs. Johnson: Until we are blue in the face. (*turns to husband*) Is my face blue?

Mr. Johnson: (*looks to her face, shakes his head 'no'*) No, just a bit pasty, my dear. (*looks at Waite*) But they need to know that you were held in the highest esteem by the citizens of this community.

Waite: I kept myself busy, all right. I was the Justice of the Peace for seventeen. This used to be my office (*open arms toward the walls*). I buried myself in the Republican party as a frequent delegate to Congressional conventions and was even the Chairman of the District convention. I also served as Supervisor and Highway Commissioner, the Secretary of the Fenton Union Agricultural Association, and was a 26-year member of the Masonic fraternity. I gave up farming after the death of my wife in 1888. I took some time to visit my sons. One lived in Kalamazoo and the other in the Upper Peninsula. I was gone from Fenton for three years but returned to open a hardware store where my office once stood.

Mrs. Johnson: You forgot to tell them about your second wife.

<u>Waite</u>: Yes, Myra Thompkinson. She was 16 years my younger and a good wife who cared for me during my old age. I died at the age of 85 in January of 1916. She died in the same year.

<u>Mrs. Johnson</u>: Tell them why your spirit remains here.

<u>Mr. Johnson</u>: Hush, he's getting to it.

<u>Waite</u>: My death certificate says I died from senility, but in truth, the grippe set in. I suffered for three days before I passed away. Myra watched over me until I took my last breath. Senility took my mind, but my memory remained. All I could think about was coming back to my office. I still believed I was the Justice of the Peace. Once I passed away, my spirit knew where it wanted to be. So here I am.

<u>Mrs. Johnson</u>: Now confess, you like to play tricks on people.

<u>Waite</u>: (*smiles and chuckles*) Yes, it is a pastime of mine. Other than these two (*nods head in Mr. & Mrs. Johnson's direction*), the conversation gets a little dull around here. I like to follow a customer as they stroll the aisles of this establishment. After they pass a book, I knock it off the shelf, and it makes a loud bang on the floor behind them. It startles some of them and brings a smile to my face as they look around innocently, knowing they didn't touch the book. I watch as they pick it up off the floor and return it to the shelf or read the back cover to see if it is a book they may be interested in purchasing.

Mr. Johnson: I must admit it is pretty funny (*chuckles*).

Waite: Sometimes, when the owner is alone, I push a poster from the top of the bookcase or decide to smoke my cigar and blow the smoke in her face.

Mrs. Johnson: I dislike the smell of his cigar (*makes a repulsive face*), so I pester him until he snuffs it out.

Waite: So, if you dare, take a turn about the store and see if I pay you a visit. I guarantee, nothing has been rigged. If a book should fall from the shelf, you know it was me who did it. (*laugh and retreat to the back of the store*)

The Lost Child

Cast:

Louise Cheney – seven-year-old lost girl
Mrs. Dustin Cheney – mother
R. Winchell – worked in Dibble's mill

Scene:

On the front porch of the big white house on Shiawassee. Little Louise is missing. Mrs. Cheney is pacing in her night dress with her shawl over her shoulders. It is 2:00 AM.

Props:

None.

Mrs. Cheney: (*looks at the night sky as she enters the stage, wraps shawl tightly around shoulders*) Can't sleep. I guess it's a mother's duty to worry. Three days. (*pacing, wringing hands, shaking head in doubt*) It's been three days. How is a seven-year-old supposed to survive alone in the wilderness? Where can she be? (*stops pacing and turns to audience*) Oh, are you here to help search for my daughter, Louise? I'm Mrs. Cheney. My husband, myself, and our eight children live in the log cabin on the corner. (*point to Phillips house*) About two years ago, Clark Dibble stumbled upon this parcel and purchased the 40 acres from the government.

He went to Grumlaw, you know it as Grand Blanc, and convinced us to move here. I won't kid you; pioneer living is a rough life. We live here amongst the Indians in Dibbleville and survive off the land. Mr. Dibble owns the small sawmill at the dam. Some of the men in this area work for him. (*resume pacing*) Where could that child be? Oh, that day haunts my mind. I had taken some of my older children with me to search for a suitable place to plant corn. Louise tried to follow us, but I told her to go back home. That child, such an inquisitive and independent one, didn't listen and wandered off. Maybe she thought to find a spot for the corn on her own. When we realized she was missing, our cry went out as 'Lost! Lost!' and was heard by neighboring towns. Those willing to join in the search arrived from Grand Blanc, Groveland, Holly, and White Lake. They gathered in the town square, behind you there (*point to Freedom Park*), and assigned areas for men to search. I've been praying to the Lord, but so far, my prayers remain unanswered. Now, Louise is a sharp girl, resourceful too, so I'm trying to remain positive and hope she will be found alive.

<u>Louise</u>: Mama!

<u>Mrs. Cheney</u>: Louise!

<u>Winchell</u>: (*carrying Louise in his arms, sets her down before her mother*)

Mrs. Cheney: (*embraces her daughter, looks to Winchell*) Oh, Louise. Mr. Winchell, however did you find her?

Winchell: Well, mam, I finished working at the mill and went out hunting for the child until I nearly exhausted myself. I returned home at midnight and threw myself on the bed for some sleep. A strange thing happened. I had a dream that showed me where your little girl was. I woke up at 2 am, put on my hat, and walked to the spot I saw in my dream. There she was, no worse for wear. She's a little bit up from mosquitos, a few scrapes, and scratches, but nothing time won't heal. A clever little girl. She stayed close to a little pool of water where she could drink from time to time.

Mrs. Cheney: How far away was she?

Winchell: (point south to Denton Hill) Over a hill about a mile or two south of here.

Mrs. Cheney: Thank you so very much, Mr. Winchell. Truly, thank you.

Winchell: You're welcome, Mrs. Cheney. I'm just glad your little girl is safely home.

Mrs. Cheney: (to Louise) Do you know how lucky you are to be found?

Louise: Yes, mama.

Mrs. Cheney: Child, I don't know whether to hug or spank you. I hope you have learned your lesson to follow my direction next time I give it.

Louise: Yes, mama. I promise to never wander on my own again.

Mrs. Cheney: Let's clean you up, put salve on those bug bites, and get you something to eat. Afterward, it's off to bed with you for some rest. (*Mrs. Cheney and Louise exit*)

Winchell: Good evening, ladies and gentlemen. I hope you liked our presentation of The Lost Child. Isn't this house grand? (*refer to the white house*) In fact, many of the houses along this street were known as Phillips Row. As you learned, the Cheney log cabin was torn down by A J Phillips, and his Queen Ann-style home was built in 1891 on the corner of Shiawassee and Adelaide. Mr. Phillips was a manufacturer of wood products such as water pumps and pie safes. He later made screen doors and windows and secured a contract with the US Government to have his doors and windows installed in the White House. He was blessed with three sons and built each one of them a house. This house was built in 1904 for his son, Harry. Two doors down, the green and stone house was built in 1908 for Ashley Phillips. However, the land had to be cleared first. Mr. Fenton's house originally resided on the property and was moved to West

Street. In 1910, the white house, two doors down from Ashley's home, was built for Winfield Phillips. The house in between the Phillips brother's homes was built in 1880 by Josiah Buckbee. He was a prominent businessman and banker. It was later owned by Charles Damon, also known as Left-Handed Charlie. He was a sharpshooter and traveled with the Wild West shows. He is also the founder of the Fenton Historical Society. Now, you may wonder if any strange happenings occur with these houses. (*laughs devilishly*) I'll never tell.

Israel Buzzard

I'm Israel Buzzard. I was born in 1831. I moved from Clarkston to Fenton in 1855 and lived in a log cabin on Denton Hill Road. Farming is my trade. My land produced wheat and oats. I had a real nice orchard too. My wife, Rosilla, and I had three children.

When the call came for men to fight for the Union, I went. When it ended, I returned. I trudged from the top of Denton Hill in 1865 with my Springfield rifle over my shoulder, and my blue uniform crumpled up in my bag. I remember wondering how my wife would be after running the farm with three small children. Instead, my ears were greeted with the excited cries of my children as they yelled, "Father, Father, you're home!"

I set to building a house with ten rooms, five of them were bedrooms. It wasn't long before we had seven children in all. Well, we had to fill up the house. The log cabin was used for storage. From what I understand, the farm is designated a centennial farm by the State of Michigan. I'm mighty proud to have it so.

After my wife died, my daughter, Addie, a schoolteacher at the Germany Road School, kept house for me. I passed away in 1905.

David Colwell

My name is David Colwell. My son, David, served as a private in the Company C 8th Michigan Cavalry Regiment.

Me and my wife, Phoebe, are very proud of our son. He joined the Union at age 16 in 1864. He wanted to do the right thing for his country.

In May of that year, he contracted typhoid fever and died at the camp hospital in Mount Sterling, Kentucky. He was buried in the Lexington City Cemetery.

We had David's body brought back to Fenton. He's buried in Oakwood Cemetery. We know he is with God now.

Charles Feckenscher

I'm Charles Feckenscher. I was born in Germany in 1840, arrived in the United States in 1852, and enlisted in the Union Army at Grass Lake, Michigan, on August 7, 1862. I was 22 years old and became a drummer boy in the Company F 20th Michigan Regiment Infantry.

I suffered a rupture and received my disability discharge on February 26, 1863, in Washington D. C.

I don't like to talk much about my service.

I married my wife, Lottie, on October 23, 1867, in Wayne, Michigan. We lived in Fenton on South Holly Road and were blessed with two children: our son, Frank, and daughter, Mae.

In the late 1800s, I opened a dry goods store two doors north of the Fenton Methodist Church. My grand window displays drew customers far and wide to my store. Oh, my umbrella sale, regularly $2.00, on sale for 89 cents, was a great success! I even had the Fenton Ladies Band livening up the event. Other window displays involved monkeys, a Ferris wheel with a collection of hankies for sale, and even a midget cow. Yes, those were the days.

I passed away in 1923 and was buried in Oakwood Cemetery, Section C, Lot 77. Stop by and visit me sometime.

Adelaide Fenton

Hello, my name is Adelaide Fenton. I sometimes ask myself; just how much are we women supposed to give for the Union's cause?

My husband, Bill, known by his regiment as Col. William Fenton, is serving in the Civil War. At 54 years old, he's too old for combat.

The other day I received word that our son, Brush, was wounded in the Battle of Chantilly in Virginia. Bill is going to visit him in the hospital in Washington D. C., so I wrote my husband and told him to try and persuade our son to come home. I also asked him to resign from his commission and come home.

If that wasn't enough to worry about, our son-in-law, William McCreary, husband to our daughter, Ada, was captured by Confederate soldiers and put in Libby Prison in Virginia. Many say officers are treated just like regular soldiers. They get a sweet potato and cornbread for their once-a-day meal. Rumor has it that 100 officers dug their way out under the road and are free. Dear God! I hope William is one of them. I pray they all come home.

Dexter Horton

I'm Dexter Horton. I lived in the green house on the corner of Shiawassee and Adelaide Streets. I was born on June 24, 1836, in Groveland in Oakland County.

At age 14, I went to Albion College. I attended school in the winter and worked on the farm in the summer. When I became the age of majority, I came to Fenton, married Lavinia Losee, and we had four children.

I liked politics and took a prominent part in the election of President Lincoln. I became postmaster of Dibbleville after his inauguration. When the Civil War began, I actively recruited able-bodied men for the Union Army. In 1863, I joined the Light Horse Artillery of the Army of the Potomac. In 1864, I was appointed Captain of the U.S. Volunteers by President Lincoln and served in Tennessee, Georgia, the Atlantic campaign, and Sherman's march at sea. I earned the rank of Major. After the war, I held several offices such as postmaster, sergeant at arms of the state senate, and the state legislature.

Locally, I served on the school board as the village president and was instrumental in taking the necessary steps for our city to observe Memorial Day.

I passed away on December 28, 1901.

I believe you will be hearing from my daughter, Mrs. Charles Bussey, at the end of this tour. She has a reputation for being quite mischievous.

Dr. Isaac Wixom, MD

I heard there was a get-together of ole civil war spirits, so I thought I would attend. I'm Dr. Isaac Wixom. My service in the Civil War began on August 19, 1861. I helped General Stockton organize the 16th Michigan Infantry. I was a surgeon and successfully performed the first hip joint amputation.

On April 18, 1863, I was court-martialed. The first charge against me was for misapplication of provisions and other military stores belonging to the United States. In other words, I ate government food. I was caught eating in the mess hall in the hospital. The U. S. Government-furnished food was for the infantrymen, not medical officers. We were to furnish our own food, even though I supplied the food to the hospital. The second charge was for using one box of brandy and one box of whiskey, each containing a dozen bottles. I believe I was court-martialed because of my political views.

I helped with the founding of the University of Michigan Medical School and was instrumental in building Argentine into a town with a hotel, general store, and mill.

I moved to Fenton in 1870 and died in 1880.

The country I loved and served turned on me.

The Famous Poker Game

Cast:

Col. William F. Fenton
Robert LeRoy
Benjamin Rockwell

Scene:

The three men gathered around a table.

Props:

Three chairs
Table
Decks of cards (staged for Fenton to win, LeRoy to come in second)
Bottle of whisky
Three shot glasses
Cigars

Fenton: (*standing, smoking his cigar, whisky in hand*) Well, I have to give your father credit. He gave us some sound advice to purchase Dibbleville from Clark Dibble. With its Indian trails converging at the center of town, it's a principal thoroughfare for many folks and a line for the railroad to the western portion of the state.

LeRoy: (*sitting on the railing of the porch*) Yes. Father is a wise man. That's why he's known as a fair and reasonable judge.

Rockwell: (*leaning back in chair*) So, now that we own Dibbleville, what's our first line of business?

Fenton: To build, expand, get ready for more settlers. There will be a demand for lumber, so we need to improve Dibble's sawmill and increase production. I'll build temporary housing for my family and me. There's a spot across from Cheney's log cabin that will do just fine. I'll make the house big enough to fit 15 to 30 people so we can take in boarders until a hotel can be constructed. Once I find the land and build my permanent residence, the boarding house can be a stagecoach stop for the town.

Rockwell: A good idea. People need places to stay until they can get settled.

LeRoy: I think I'll build a general store, get my supplies from Pontiac, and employ a few people.

Rockwell: More men will be needed at the mill too.

Fenton: This town will be a hub for many travelers, with many deciding to settle here.

Rockwell: Dibbleville! (*raises glass*)

(*Fenton and LeRoy cringe*)

LeRoy: We can't call our town Dibbleville. It no longer belongs to him. And since we all bought an equal share in the town, we can't go by who owns the biggest share.

Fenton: The name should be changed, but to what? (*All quiet for a moment, smoke on cigars*)

Rockwell: (*slaps his hand on the table*) I say we do this the diplomatic way.

LeRoy: Let my father decide?

Rockwell: No. We settle this over a game of poker.

Fenton: Seven-card stud, winner take all?

Rockwell: Not quite. The best hand gets to name the town after himself. The second-best hand gets to name the main street, and the loser gets to name the main residential street.

LeRoy: So, we're leaving this up to a game of luck.

Fenton: Sounds fair to me. Deal 'em up.

(*Fenton sits at a table next to Rockwell's left. LeRoy sits in the remaining chair. Rockwell hands the deck of cards to his left. Fenton taps the deck with his knuckled hand and passes the cards back. The card game is played, drink, smoke, and react to each card dealt.*)

Rockwell: Moment of truth. Show what you got.

(*hands are revealed one at a time, Fenton celebrates*)

Fenton: Well, boys, it looks like I have the highest hand. I'll call the town Fentonville. (*raises glass*)

LeRoy: And its main street will be known as LeRoy Street. (*raises glass*)

Rockwell: Rockwell Street it is, with many fine houses lining it. (*raises glass*)

Fenton: Our good names shall leave our mark upon this town for future generations. May we be remembered as productive and contributing citizens. (*drink from glasses*) "Maybe they will make bronze statues in honor of us someday."

First Presbyterian Church
Rena Conrad

Cast:

Rena Conrad – deceased, age 19, ambitious and cheerful personality
Rev. A. G. Work – deceased pastor at the Presbyterian Church
Mrs. Myra Bussey – deceased church member
Singer

Scene:

The altar of the Presbyterian Church

Props:

Bouquet of lilies
Bible
Organ
Music

Work: (*holds open Bible or standing behind the pulpit*) We gather today to pay homage to Rena Conrad, that young woman who was struck down in the prime of her life.

Conrad: Yes, Reverend, we know. My death happened in 1911. So, we don't have to keep reliving this over and over again.

Bussey: Yes, you do. It's called a residual haunt.

(*Work and Conrad roll eyes and look to Bussey*)

Work: At the young age of 19, Miss Conrad took her last breath.

Bussey: (plays a note on the keyboard) Instead of going over the funeral for the umpteenth millionth time, why don't we talk about our lives and what we accomplished?

Conrad: (*looks to Work*) She's right.

Bussey: Of course, I'm right.

Work: (*closes Bible abruptly*)

Conrad: My name is Rena Conrad. I am, or was, a junior at Fenton High school. Perhaps you have visited my father's store, Conrad's Café. (*points northward*)

Bussey: Oh, that's been long gone. (*waves hand dismissively*)

Conrad: It was just down the road past Caroline Street on the left. Father offered delicious food. I helped him at the store from time to time.

Bussey: Go ahead. Tell them how you died. Everyone likes to know the details.

Conrad: I was diagnosed with rheumatism. I was doing well for nearly a year before my father was stricken with neuralgia of the heart. His illness upset me so that it affected my heart. My mother, with the help of Mr. Cook, had me removed from our house to his house across the street. Perhaps she thought I would be well cared for since he was our town druggist. I was put in a quiet room with a comfortable bed, where I took my last breath.

Considering my father's health, my mother thought it best to have my funeral here (*motions by spreading arms wide*) in the First Presbyterian Church instead of having it at our house.

Work: At my recommendation, that is. Even though you weren't a church member, you spent many hours serving on the Young People's Society. Your funeral is one I will never forget. You were such a popular young lady. Nearly everyone in town attended. Your mother and sister, Nellie, sat right there in the front row. (*point to a pew*)

Conrad: Unfortunately, Father was unable to attend.

Work: And that lovely bouquet of lilies. Such symbolism with each lily representing you and your friends.

Conrad: The lily that represented me was broken. Several of the young men in my junior class carried my body from Mr. Cook's house to here for the service and then to Oakwood Cemetery, where it rests in peace.

Work: And what a sermon I gave that day. (*open arms wide and look about the church*) This is where I preached. Isn't it a beautiful little church? Have you heard the bell? It's made from hard-to-come-by iron during the Civil War, transported by train from

Pennsylvania, and placed in the steeple. Since it's pretty heavy, the clapper is worn on only one side because the bell ringers lack the strength to pull the rope to make the bell swing entirely from side to side. (*sigh*) But it has rung the joyous news of God's calling over the years.

Bussey: In the 1930s, I was instrumental in leading the Social Circle to raise money for the church's restoration. We updated the parlors, school room, kitchen and heat, and even this beautiful organ. (*runs a hand across its top, pressing a key or two*) I like to press a key on it from time to time just to remind everyone that I'm still here.

Work: Your work on the committee was greatly appreciated by the congregation.

Conrad: We have all contributed in our own way. This is a good town with kind people. They even remembered to sing my favorite hymn at my funeral, "Beautiful Isle of Somewhere." (*Beautiful Isle of Somewhere is performed*)

101 West Rockwell Street

<u>Cast</u>:

John B. Hamilton – former resident
Miss Alice Van Atta – piano teacher

<u>Scene</u>:

Front porch

<u>Props</u>:

Clothing for the time period

<u>John</u>: Good evening, ladies and gentlemen. I'm John Hamilton. Let me tell you about this house and its history. After the death of Elisha Holmes in 1854, I purchased at an auction this lot, which is Lot 1, and lots 7 and part of 8, which line LeRoy Street. I had to wait two years before acquiring the property because it was in probate. Initially, a house was located on Lot 7 (*point behind the house to the next lot*), and this lot contained a carriage house. In 1902, I sold lots 7 and 8 and built this house. Some of you may know it by its nickname - the Honey House. My wife, Charlotte, and I love bees. As many of you know, they have an essential role in our agriculture. During the summer months, Charlotte had plenty of flowers for them to gather their food. They made the sweetest honey in the

county, and the children of Fenton knew it too. Charlotte would take the time to put honey in small jars, and we would hand them out as Halloween treats. (*glance at the length of the house*) My house isn't quite as I remember it. The front door used to face LeRoy Street, and the opposite end of the house contained a porch. Our front room had a piano that was widely used by children in town. (*smile toward Alice*)

Alice: Yes, indeed. I'm Miss Alice Van Atta, known by many as the piano teacher. The Hamiltons allowed me to give lessons in their home during winter when walking up an icy and snowy hill in leather shoes was a challenge for my students. I remember one student, in particular, who came to his lesson with a terrible cough. I think Mr. Hamilton grew tired of listening to his rattling. So he went to the kitchen, heated up some honey, and gave it to the student to soothe his throat. Well, once word got out about the tasty remedy, many of my students acquired a cough, and others took a sudden interest in learning the piano.

John: I remember the children, so cold from walking. But back then, most people walked to get to where they needed. Many had carriages in their carriage houses but no horses. It was easier to rent a horse than maintain one. There were four liveries in town. The closest was on Shiawassee just west of Andrew's block. I believe there is a banquet room there now. The Laundry Room? Another was northwest of A J Phillips's business office on Mill

Street, just past today's post office. The largest livery was on the corner of Roberts and River Streets, where the State Back now resides. And the last one was across the street from the Fenton Hotel, where Fenton Glass is today. Even though we had plenty of liveries, a person had to walk to rent the horse, ride it back to their carriage house, and hitch it up before taking their trip. Then once they returned, they had to ride the horse back to the livery and walk home. (*steps forward, lower voice to emphasize the unknown*) Some say on a quiet night, the clip-clopping of a horse-drawn carriage can still be heard. Even though I died over 100 years ago, my spirit still resides within this house. For a while, a young lady lived here by herself. I wanted to reassure her that she wasn't alone. I turned on her shower in the upstairs bathroom while she sat in her living room. When she was away, I pushed her books toward the back of each shelf of her bookcase. (*chuckle*) She likes to keep them all the way forward, so she doesn't have to dust them. I think her dog can see me. It peeks around her and stares at me when I'm standing behind her and won't go into the basement when I'm down there. I made the mistake of appearing before a child while she was once having a party. He described me as the blue man. Maybe he was referring to my clothing. Chester, our son, inherited the house upon our passing.

Alice: Chester allowed me to continue my piano lessons. (*turn toward John*) Such a fine son you had.

John: Thank you. My wife and I are buried in Oakwood Cemetery in Section M.

Alice: Not only did I experience John's passing, but his son's too. I lived to be 100 years old. I'm buried in section H.

711 South LeRoy Street

Cast:

George Marion Eddy – 75 years old when he passed away in 1910
Miss Maude Morris – spinster, passed away in 1955 at age 67

Scene:

Garden behind the garage

Props:

Proper clothing for the time period of the character's life

George: Good evening, ladies and gentlemen. I'm George Marion Eddy. My family can date our history back to the Mayflower when Samuel Eddy immigrated to America, landing in Plymouth, Massachusetts, on October 29, 1630.

I was born in 1834 in Erie, Pennsylvania, and came to Fentonville with my parents in 1837. Our farm was north of town.

In 1856, I married Jane McOmber. We have three beautiful children. Unfortunately, my wife died in our home 33 years later at age 54.

In 1889, I went to Muskegon, purchased an abandoned car line, and brought the rails back to Fenton. After receiving the city's approval, I laid the tracks from my livery, located across from the Fenton Hotel to Long Lake. The lake is known as Lake Fenton today. I owned and operated the first streetcar trolley in Genesee County. The trolley took you to my lakefront cottage with its wraparound porch. It was known as Eddy's Landing. We served food, provided boat rides, and rented cottages and boats. My 12 horses were used to pull the several trolley cars to and from the lake. My first day in business was on July 4, 1891. Much to my delight, I had 2000 people use the trolley system that day. It was a grand celebration with a women's band entertaining everyone too. You may have heard of the boats I owned – 'The City of Fenton' and 'The City of Flint' - that toured the lake. Each steamer could carry 750 passengers.

I married my second wife, Hattie Wells, in 1891. We lived on the farm during our marriage. My health began to fail in my old age. I was diagnosed with uremic poisoning. Dang, kidneys just didn't want to work anymore. I sold my business to George Bridson before my passing in 1910. My wife moved to this house and lived here until her passing thirty years later, on October 10, 1940.

Maude: I received word of my Aunt Hattie passing by letter. She had bequeathed this lovely house to me. So, I packed up my belongings, traveled from

New York City, and remained in residence until my passing in 1955.

I took a particular interest in this house. You see, James E. Bussey built it in the 1860s. He owned a hardware store in town and helped his father-in-law with his manufacturing company. He and his wife, Mary, had five children. I believe they lived here for 30 years or so before moving into the house down the road.

I never married but enjoyed my life of solitude. I was raised to be a proper lady. When preparing my afternoon tea, I sat at a small table in the front living room window with two servings of scones, cookies, and sometimes even cake on a small plate. I set an extra cup, saucer, and plate in case someone dropped by to visit and enjoy a cup of tea with me. If you happen to see my little table set for tea and me in the window, be sure to stop by for a visit.

308 South Holly Road

Cast:

Charles W. Coe – known as 'C. W.', born in England.
Grace Bussey Gurnea – granddaughter of C. W. Coe

Scene:

Front porch

Props:

Proper dress for the time period

Coe: Welcome to my home! I'm Charles W. Coe, and I built this house in 1870. (*spreads arms wide*) It's impressive, two and a half stories high. There was a small house to the east (*motion toward East Street*) where my sister, Kate, and her husband lived until her death. As you can see, it no longer exists.

A little about me. I was born in England in 1818. I was the youngest of three sons. At a young age, I came to New York City, where I learned the blacksmithing trade. I left New York and settled in Ingham County, where I purchased 1100 acres and opened a dry goods business. It was a life lesson indeed, for the business failed. I moved to Corunna,

Michigan, bought a lot, and erected a store and residence. On November 7, 1861, at age 43, I enlisted in Michigan 1st Calvary Battalion, Company H. My daughter, Mary, was wed to James Bussey on December 31 of that same year. I was honored to serve under Brigadier General George Armstrong Custer at the Battle of Gettysburg. I saw many men fall during the 10 battles I fought. I returned home at the war's end and resumed working in my business. Shortly afterward, a fire destroyed the building. I sold the lot, and we moved to Fenton, where I returned to my blacksmithing trade. I invented the first power drill operated by hand, improved it over time, sold it throughout the United States, and exported them to Prussia, Russia, and England. Others tried to infringe on my patents. My case was finally tried by the Supreme Court of the United States and ruled in my favor. I built a factory on Mill Pond near East Shiawassee and South Oak streets. It manufactured drills, twist drills, tire-up-setters, and tire binders. I passed away on July 16, 1888. My son-in-law took over the running of my factory and ran a hardware store too. Once my wife, Ann, passed away in 1897, Mary, our daughter, and her husband, James, inherited this house and updated it in the Victorian style. They added the wrap-around porch, tower, bay windows, and kitchen with its west side entrance. James installed gas lighting and had a tank filled with gasoline. A large pressure cylinder in the backyard created a mixture of gas, sent it into the house, and through the pipes. It was the first house to have gas lighting in Fenton. I don't remember the iron fencing. (*glance at it*) I suspect he made it in the foundry too. Nice.

Ah, further accolades I received, I was a member of the Episcopal Church and one of the oldest members of the Fenton Commandery of Knights Templar and the Sovereign Consistory of Detroit. My wife and I are buried in Section E of Oakwood Cemetery.

<u>Grace</u>: Hello, I'm Grace Bussey Gurnea. By the way, my family's name is actually De Bussey. I'm the oldest of James and Mary's children. My husband passed away shortly after we were married. I never remarried. I lived here in my grandfather's house (*motion to Coe*) and cared for my mother, Mary, who inherited the house after my grandmother, Ann, passed away. Mother was quite ill for the last two years of her life. I recall her sitting in a chair staring into the front room (*motion to the picture window*). The large oak pocket doors were open. She babbled about many people in the room and a man dressed in uniform standing guard in the corner. The people would enter through one door and exit out the other. (*point to the front entrance on the west side of the house and then to the east side*) The door on the east side was removed during renovations.

<u>Coe</u>: Well, my dear granddaughter, she was describing my viewing. I was laid out in a casket in the front room. People would enter the west door and exit the east door. Since I served in the military,

an Honor Guard stood to watch over my body to let the living know that my service was appreciated and would not be forgotten.

Grace: After my mother passed away, the house was deeded to me by my three siblings. Once I passed, it was willed to my youngest brother, Charles, who sold the house. It had been in our family for 90 years. Since then, many families have enjoyed its splendor. During a renovation, an account ledger and rosary were discovered in one of the exterior walls, and two small cement caskets were found beneath the ground. They are sealed with cement tops. One is absent of markings, while the other has the word baby written in stone on its lid. It is uncertain if what lies inside are children who died at a young age or perhaps family pets. You are more than welcome to tour the flower garden where they lie at rest. (*motion toward the garden*)

Coe: It's right that way, don't be shy, step right that way. (point toward the garden)

305 Rockwell Street

Cast:

Fritz E. Jeudevine: 55 years old when he passed away in 1938
Horace Carter Churchill: 84 years old, passed away in 2008

Scene:

Front porch.

Props:

Proper clothing for time period of character's life.

Jeudevine: I am Fritz E. Jeudevine. This grand house was built in 1860 by James R. Burdick Potter. His wife was Frances McLean Potter. They had three children. Mrs. Potter passed away a year after giving birth to their youngest child, Joshua. Mr. Potter owned a saddlery and harness business in town. He and his wife, Joshua, and other relatives are buried in the family plot in section E of Oakwood Cemetery.

I was born in South Dakota on October 25, 1883. My parents, George and Effie, my two brothers, sister, and I came to Fenton when I was 21 years old. My father owned a local grocery and meat market. He came up with the slogan 'me want beans.' Since it was a family business, I worked in our store. When I was 55, I went to see my sister, who was married and lived in Kalamazoo. Unfortunately, I passed away while there. My body was brought back to Fenton, laid in state inside this house, and a funeral was conducted by George A. Monroe. He was from Flint and presided over my Christian Science service. I am also buried in the Oakwood Cemetery, section D, if you ever care to pay your respects.

Churchill: I'm Horace Carter Churchill. Many just called me Carter. This was my house, or shall I say it still is? I was born in Hinsdale, Illinois, in 1924 and moved to Fenton in 1937. I served in WWII from February 1943 to 1946. I was a lifetime member of the VFW here in town, UAW 659, and the Durant Depot Preservation Group. I worked at the Chevrolet Plant #4 and V-8 Engine and retired after 30 years of employment in 1976. I cared for my mother until her death and attended antique car shows as a hobby. I never married and didn't mind living alone. Toward the end of my life, many in town thought I was losing my mind when I loaned my caretaker $69,000. One day I asked when she had planned to pay me back. She called me senile and said we had no such agreement for her to repay the money. Not sure what she did with my money, but I knew she liked to drink the hard stuff. (*motion as if drinking from a bottle*) As I grew older, it was frustrating to watch my home deteriorate as I could not do the upkeep on it. The people who live here now are doing an excellent job. I'm pleased to see the progress and changes they're making. I like to let them know I'm still around, though, keeping an eye on what they're doing. One night when the woman was watching TV, I flipped her ponytail and tapped her on the head. Then there was the day I watched her from the kitchen doorway. She entered the dining room, and I had to turn quickly before she walked through me. I heard her claim she saw my apparition. Well, part of me anyway, from my waist down like a pair of pants suspended in the air with nobody inside them. She even described my pockets as being square. Oh, I watch over her and her husband as well. One night when they went to bed, they left a candle burning. I blew it out. I don't want to see their restoration work go up in smoke. I spent the last days of my life at the Argentine Care Center in Linden until I passed away in 2008. My grave can be found at the Great Lakes National Cemetery in Holly, MI.

407 Pine Street

<u>Cast</u>:

Henry Clay Riggs – druggist/lawyer
Rite D. Dedrick – son of John W. Dedrick, farmer and carpenter

<u>Scene</u>:

Front porch

<u>Props</u>:

Time period clothing – late 1800s, early 1900s

<u>Dedrick</u>: Hello, ladies and gentlemen. My name is Rite D. Dedrick. My father, John, sold our farm in New York and moved my mother, Elizabeth, my younger brother, Frank, and me to Fentonville shortly after the 1860 census. Frank passed away at the age of three in 1861. He is buried in Oakwood Cemetery on Prospect Hill. Dad, a natural carpenter, built this house in the 1860s. He enlisted in Company H, the 11th Michigan Infantry, in February of 1865, fought and returned after the end of the Civil War. My little brother, John B., was born in 1867. In 1870, I married Emma Eugenia Garner, a Fenton resident. Between 1873 and 1880, Dad sold the house, and we moved to Baker, Kansas. I earned my living just like Dad – farming and carpentry. Mom passed away in 1891 and is buried

in Mt. Olive Cemetery in Pittsburg, Kansas. I can't remember when my dad died, but in 1900 my wife and I moved to Oregon for a time. It was easy to pick up and go, you see, we never had any children. We eventually returned to Kansas. My dear Emma passed away in November of 1932. I joined her in eternal rest a month later. We are buried at the same cemetery as my father, the Swars Prairie Baptist Cemetery in Seneca, Missouri.

<u>Riggs</u>: My name is Henry Clay Riggs, druggist and attorney at law. I remember when this grand old house was built. Rumor has it that it broke the bank. However, my name is on the paperwork indicating I provided the mortgages to John. You see, banks back then weren't insured. They were privately owned, and some owners couldn't be trusted. Over the years, several banks in Fentonville folded. Did you ever hear about the owners of the Trump and Wilmot Bank? No? It was owned by Edwin Trump and George Washington Wilmot. They nearly broke their bank over a silly competition to see who could build the most magnificent house in town. I believe the year was 1867. I'm sure you know the houses I'm referencing. Wilmot's house is the big white house on the southeast corner of East and Rockwell. Trump's house is located on the southeast corner of East and High streets. I believe Trump's house is larger with a third story that once held a gym. Anyway, a wealthy German farmer by the name of Holtforth was impressed by Wilmot's house and decided he wanted to build big, beautiful houses too. He withdrew all of his money from his

bank. Once word got out, people panicked. Everyone withdrew their money from the bank, causing its collapse. Now in town, you may have noticed the camera shop was once a bank, the Commercial State Savings Bank to be exact, not to be confused with The State Bank, which was later established in 1897. Rest assured, whichever bank your money resides in today, it's safe. Or so they say. (*grin*)

206 Rockwell Street

Cast:

Caroline LeRoy St Amand – 33 years old at time of death in 1847, first wife
Emily Stene (Steere, Stew) St Amand – second wife

Scene:

Standing on the front porch.

Props:

Period clothing.

Caroline: I'm Caroline LeRoy St Amand, sister of Robert LeRoy and daughter of Judge Daniel LeRoy. Many of you may know that my brother and Col. William Fenton purchased Dibbleville from Clark and Wallace Dibble in 1837.

I met my husband while traveling southward with my father on the Saginaw Turnpike near Springfield. Today that road is known as Dixie Highway. But oh, bother, our carriage had broken down. We were stranded. I'll admit, I was in a bit of a tizzy. Even though I was accompanied by my father, I didn't like to be in the wild with so many animals and Indians. Well, one never knows. (*shudder*) Much to our delight, or mine rather, came a man, a very handsome man, traveling in the opposite direction. He reined his horse to a halt, hopped down from his wagon, and helped my father make the necessary repairs to our carriage. (*sigh*) Such a gallant gesture. Chivalric too. He spoke only when we departed for our home in Pontiac, and he said, "Au revoir." Augustus St Amand came to this country from Paris, France, after inheriting a third of a million dollars. He arrived in New Orleans, traveled up the Mississippi River, purchased a plot of land from a friend on Byram Lake, and built a log cabin. He was traveling from Detroit after obtaining supplies when he came upon us. Ah, divine intervention. I like to believe he searched his heart upon our meeting and fell in love. We were married in Fentonville on February 5th, 1839, and lived in this lovely house built by my brother and Col. Fenton when it was completed in 1842. It was only four rooms then - two downstairs and two upstairs. We were blessed with four children during our eight years of marriage – Augustus, who served our country and died of typhoid fever during the Civil War, Fernenard, Leroy, and Caroline Emma. I passed away in one of the upstairs bedrooms in 1847, just eleven days after giving birth to little Caroline, who died three months later. I'm buried in our family plot in Old Prospect Hill, the oldest section of Oakwood Cemetery. My gravestone is written in French, where I rest in peace.

<u>Emily</u>: I'm Emily, Augustus's second wife. I was visiting the Fentons when I met Augustus. We married in May of 1848 and lived in Flint. Our home

was blessed with the birth of our daughter, Caroline Emily. I was left with all four children and one on the way when my husband abruptly left his job in 1851 as the treasurer for Genessee County and went to France on urgent business. Shortly afterward, the township books were discovered to be out of balance. Robert L. Sheldon and Col. William M. Fenton replaced the missing funds with their own money. In my husband's defense, Augustus tried to obtain the remainder of his inheritance from a reverend in the convent where he was educated. Before he left, Augustus told me when he attended the convent as a child, he rarely saw his parents even though they lived near it. During his absence, I heard rumors that my husband had lost his money through lousy land investments. I was worried sick, for I received no communication, no letters while he was abroad. He returned empty-handed. The clerk at the convent told him that the reverend had confiscated the remainder of his inheritance. Our son, Earnest, was born in December of 1851. To this day, I believe the child's poor health is due to my worried state while my husband was away. We moved to Wallsville, Pennsylvania, shortly after my husband's return from abroad.

First Presbyterian Church

Cast:

Choir Master
Choir

Scene:

Altar of church

Props:

Choir robes

Choir Master: The Civil War was a trying time for our country. Many believe the war was an issue about slavery, but that is only partially true. You see, the succession of the South resulted from the decision to make newly acquired land west of the Mississippi River 'slave-free.' President Abraham Lincoln did not want to take the slaves away from the South because he knew they were vital to its economy. But once the South succeeded, he was determined to keep the country united and wrote the Emancipation Proclamation. It did not free the slaves but gave the Union soldiers the authority to confiscate southern slaves, bring them northward, and set them free. Many slaves risked their lives by escaping and traveling at night to safehouses dotted along the way as they traveled northward through the Underground Railroad. They would look for a quilt displayed in an attic window, a star on a wall of the house, or the lit lantern of a jockey statue, indicating it was a place they could rest their head during the day before traveling the next leg of their journey. A stop along the underground railroad included this lovely town of Fentonville. After a slave crossed over into Canada, many rejoiced with others who, for the first time in their lives, tasted freedom and celebrated in song. (*perform song*)

Jokes

Q: Why do demons and ghouls hang out together?
A: Because demons are a ghoul's best friend.

Q: Why are vampires like false teeth?
A: They both come out at night.

Q: What is a witch's favorite subject in school?
A: Spelling.

Q: Why don't mummies take a vacation?
A: They are afraid to relax and unwind.

Q: What do you call a monster who poisons corn flakes?
A: A cereal killer.

Q: Why do ghosts like to ride in elevators?
A: It raises their spirits.

Q: Why does a cemetery have to keep a fence around it?
A: Because people are dying to get in.

Q: What do you have to take to become a coroner?
A: A stiff exam.

Q: Why don't ghosts go out in the rain?
A: It dampens their spirits.

Q: What is a ghost's favorite kind of street?
A: A dead end.

Q: What do little ghosts drink?
A: Evaporated milk.

Q: Why are so few ghosts arrested?
A: It's hard to pin anything on them.

Q: Where do hard working ghosts go on vacation?
A: The Eerie Canal.

Q: Why are ghosts so bad at lying?
A: Because you can see right through them.

Q: What is a vampire's favorite fruit?
A: A nectarine.

Q: Why did the vampire read the Wall Street Journal?
A: He heard it had great circulation.

Q: Who did the scary ghost invite to his party?
A: Any old friend he could dig up.

Q: What is a mummy's favorite music?
A: Wrap.

Q: What do you call a ghost in a torn sheet?
A: A holy terror.

Q: Why do mummies have trouble keeping friends?
A: They are too wrapped up in themselves.

Q: What did the farmer say to the scarecrow?
A: "I'll keep you posted."

Q: Why is a cemetery a great place to write a story?
A: Because there are so many plots.

Q: Why are spiders such good baseball players?
A: They know how to catch flies.

Q: What happened to the guy who couldn't keep up his payments to the exorcist?
A: He was repossessed.

Q: What kind of streets do zombies like?
A: Dead ends.

Q: Why doesn't the scarecrow eat much?
A: He's already stuffed.

Q: What do you get when you cross a spider with an ear of corn?
A: Cobwebs.

Q: What is a zombie's favorite dessert?
A: Ladyfingers.

Q: Why did the headless horseman go into business?
A: He wanted to get ahead in life.

Q: Why are skeletons so calm?
A: Because nothing gets under their skin.

Q: What kind of boat pulls Dracula when he water skis?
A: A blood vessel.

Q: What is a skeleton's favorite musical instrument?
A: A trom-bone.

Thank you for reading

The Fenton Ghost Walk Revisited

If you have a moment, please share your review with others and post on social media.

For additional information about the author, signings, and her books, please visit

www.BrendaHasseBooks.com

To sign-up for the author's newsletter, please visit

www.BrendaHasseBooks.com/newsletter-sign-up

CPSIA information can be obtained
at www.ICGtesting.com
Printed in the USA
LVHW081917220722
723880LV00012B/482

9 798986 438313